Native Americans

The Seminole

Richard M. Gaines

ABDO Publishing Company

visit us at
www.abdopub.com

Published by ABDO Publishing Company, 4940 Viking Drive, Suite 622, Edina, Minnesota 55435. Copyright © 2000 Abdo Consulting Group, Inc., Pentagon Tower, P.O. Box 36036, Minneapolis, Minnesota 55435 USA. International copyrights reserved in all countries. No part of this book may be reproduced in any form without written permission from the publisher.

Printed in the United States.

Illustrator: David Kanietakeron Fadden
Cover Photo: Corbis
Interior Photos: Corbis
Editors: Bob Italia, Tamara L. Britton, Kate A. Furlong
Art Direction & Maps: Pat Laurel
Border Design: Carey Molter/MacLean & Tuminelly (Mpls.)

Library of Congress Cataloging-in-Publication Data

Gaines, Richard M., 1942-
   The Seminole/ Richard M. Gaines.
      p. cm. -- (Native Americans)
   Includes bibliographical references and index.
   Summary: Presents a brief introduction to the Seminole Indians including information on their society, homes, food, clothing, crafts, and life today.
   ISBN 1-57765-376-9
   1. Seminole Indians--Juvenile literature. [1. Seminole Indians. 2. Indians of North America--Florida.] I. Title.

E99.S28 G35 2000
975.9'004973--dc21

                                  99-059871

Contributing Editor: Barbara Gray, JD

Barbara Gray, JD (Kanatiyosh) is a member of the Mohawk Nation (Akwesasne), which is in New York State and Canada. Barbara earned her Juris Doctorate from Arizona State University College of Law in May of 1999. She is presently pursuing a Doctorate in Justice Studies that focuses on American Indian culture and issues at Arizona State University. When she finishes school, she will return home to the Mohawk Nation.

Illustrator: David Kanietakeron Fadden

David Kanietakeron Fadden is a member of the Akwesasne Mohawk Wolf Clan. His work has appeared in publications such as *Akwesasne Notes, Indian Time,* and the *Northeast Indian Quarterly.* Examples of his work have also appeared in various publications of the Six Nations Indian Museum in Onchiota, NY. His work has also appeared in "How The West Was Lost: Always The Enemy," produced by Gannett Production which appeared on the Discovery Channel. David's work has been exhibited in Albany, NY; the Lake Placid Center for the Arts; Centre Strathearn in Montreal, Quebec; North Country Community College in Saranac Lake, NY; Paul Smith's College in Paul Smiths, NY; and at the Unison Arts & Learning Center in New Paltz, NY.

Contents

Where They Lived

The Seminole's original homelands included a large part of the southeastern United States. It included present-day Georgia, Alabama, South Carolina, Tennessee, Mississippi, and Florida. They shared this land with many tribes who spoke the *maskoki* language.

When English traders met these tribes, they mistakenly called them Creek. That is why many books say the Seminole came from Creeks. This is only partly true. The Seminole actually came from many different native peoples who lived in the region.

The Florida Everglades

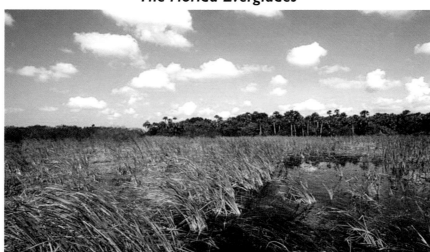

These native people called themselves *yat'siminoli*. It means the "free people." In the 1770s, the English began to call these native people the Seminole.

In the 1700s, the U.S. government tried to force the Seminole from their homelands. When the U.S. Army attacked, the Seminole escaped into the **Everglades**.

During the days of slavery, the Seminole welcomed runaway slaves to live alongside them. The slaves shared the Seminole's common gardens. But, they lived in their own villages.

In the mid-1800s, the U.S. government forced many Seminole onto a **reservation** in Oklahoma. Some Seminole escaped into the Florida swampland. Today, many Seminole remain in Florida.

The Seminole
Homelands

EVERGLADES

5

Society

The Seminole built villages on **Everglade** islands called hammocks. Hammocks could be reached by canoe only. Hammocks had hardwood cypress and palmetto trees, and sawgrass. They also had good soil for planting gardens.

The Seminole built their homes around the island's outside edge. In the center, they built a cook house and an eating house. Guests stayed in the eating house.

The **traditional** teachings hold Seminole society together. These teachings contain the instructions on how to live in harmony with nature.

The Green Corn Dance is a special Seminole ceremony. Villages gather to thank the Creator for keeping balance and harmony between people and nature.

During the Green Corn Dance, men and women split into different camps. Each camp has people from its own **clan**. They participate in different **rituals**.

One **ritual** is the stomp dance. The dancers follow in a single-file row behind the leader. The leader weaves in and out like a snake moving along the ground. As he dances, he sings. At certain points in the song, the men answer him.

A Seminole village on a hammock

Homes

When the Seminole lived in northern Florida, they built log homes. Sometimes, the homes were two stories tall.

In the 1800s, the U.S. Army attacked the Seminole. To escape from the troops, the Seminole moved deeper into the swamps. It was hard to build log homes in the swampland. So, the Seminole began to build *chickees*. *Chickee* is the Seminole word for house.

Chickees are open-aired homes. Usually, they had no walls. A cooling breeze could reach the family from all sides and from below. Thatch covered the *chickee's* slanted roof.

The Seminole built *chickees* from cypress logs. *Chickees* were about 16 feet (5 m) long, 9 feet (3 m) wide, and 12 feet (3.6 m) high. Four large, standing logs formed the main frame. Smaller logs completed the frame. Vines held the frame together.

Vines also held the *chickee* platform to the frame. Platforms were often built 3 feet (1 m) off the ground. This kept the *chickees* from flooding during the rainy season. It also kept the people safe from alligators.

At night, the family slept on the platform. During the day, they stored their bedding in the **rafters**. Then, they used the platform for everyday living.

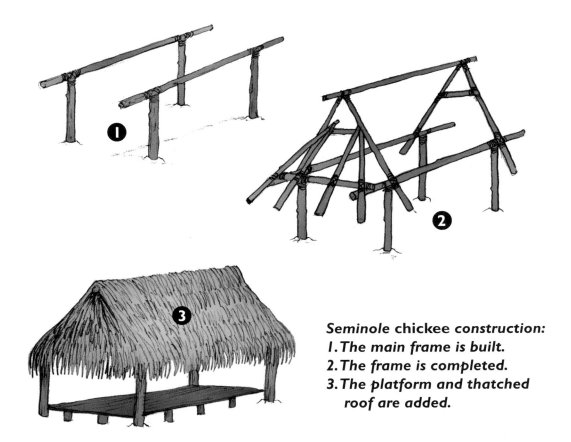

Seminole **chickee** *construction:*
1. The main frame is built.
2. The frame is completed.
3. The platform and thatched roof are added.

Food

The Seminole gardened, hunted, fished, and gathered wild plants. The Seminole gardens contained melons, squash, pumpkins, corn, and beans. Their main crop was corn. They boiled the corn and made **hominy**.

The men hunted and trapped. They used bows and arrows and blow guns. Men hunted game such as turkey, duck, deer, bear, and alligator. The men also fished in the nearby rivers and swamps. The game, fish, and fowl were smoked over a fire. This **preserved** the meats for later use.

The women gathered wild fruits, nuts, and greens. They also searched for arrowroot plants. They pounded the arrowroot's underground stalks into flour.

The Seminole made fruit drinks. A special drink called *sofki* was made from roasted corn or hominy.

In the village center, the Seminole built a cooking house and an eating house. All the families shared these buildings.

Food was cooked on a fire. It was raised on a large earthen platform. The fire logs were arranged like the spokes of a wheel. As they burned, they were pushed towards the center to make the fire burn longer.

The Seminole had no set time to eat. In the camp's center, a pot of soup was kept warm over the fire pit. People ate when they were hungry.

The Seminole traded with Europeans for food and goods. They traded feathers, alligator hides, and deer hides for flour, sugar, coffee, metal pots, beads, guns, and cloth.

Later, the Seminole began to farm. They owned cattle and pigs.

A Seminole cooking house

Clothing

When the Seminole lived north of Florida, they wore deerskin clothes. The men wore leggings and **breechcloths**. The women wore leather dresses and moccasins. In the winter, men and women wore fur robes. Everyone wore moccasins.

The Seminole who lived in Florida wore clothing made from plants and animals. Women wore skirts made of tree moss or **palmetto fronds**. Some wore deerskin shirts. Over their shirts, women wore **mantles** of woven palmetto leaves. In cooler weather, women added a short, deerskin wrap or shawl.

The men wore breechcloths made of woven or braided palmetto leaves. For special occasions, the men wore colorful cloaks made of feathers.

Men and women often went barefoot. Sometimes, they wore moccasins. They also wore hats made of woven palmetto leaves or bird feathers. And, they carried bags made of woven palmetto leaves and other grasses.

Boys were naked until they were 12 to 15 years old. Then, they wore **breechcloths**. Young girls wore the same kind of clothing as their mothers.

The Seminole wore beads made of copper, gold, pearls, and fish and animal bones. They often tattooed their bodies. Sometimes, the women wore many beaded necklaces. The beads covered the neck up to the ears and could weigh almost 15 pounds (7 kg).

In the late 1800s, the Seminole traded with Europeans for cloth. The women began to make dresses, shirts, and blouses. They hand sewed **calico** cloth strips of solid colors. This made an artistic design for which the Seminole became famous.

A Seminole family in traditional dress

Crafts

Seminole men made dugout canoes. Canoes were needed to travel in the **Everglades**. First, the men selected a tall, straight cypress tree. Then, they cut down the tree, sometimes with fire.

Sometimes, the tree trunk was too heavy to move. The men had to wait until the rainy season to move it. Then, the trunk could be floated on the water.

The men carved the outside of the logs into a canoe shape. Then, they used axes and even fire to hollow it out.

The men also made **pendants**. To do this, men pounded silver coins into a **crescent** shape.

Seminole women wove baskets and mats. They used cane and palmetto stalks. Baskets stored food. Woven mats were slept on.

In the 1920s, the Seminole began to sell items to tourists. The women made extra patchwork clothing and dolls. The dolls were made from **palmetto fiber** and stuffed with cotton. The dolls wore clothing made of colorful patchwork. The dolls also wore the hairstyles of the men and women.

A Seminole man builds a
canoe with tools and fire.

Family

Clans are important to Seminole society. The clans are named after things in nature. The clans link people and nature to form one big family.

At one time, the Seminole had many clans. But today, only eight clans remain. The eight Seminole clans are the Panther, Wind, Bear, Deer, Bird, Snake, Toad (or Big Town), and Otter.

The Seminole are a matrilineal society. This means clans are passed from mother to child. A clan becomes **extinct** when the last woman of the clan dies.

People may not marry someone in their own clan. People of the same clan are considered family.

When a couple married, they moved to a new *chickee* within the village. Everyone made sure that the couple was safe and happy.

The village was like one big family. People ate together. At night, the **elders** told stories. Some stories were **legends** and **myths**. Other stories told about Seminole history and **culture**.

A Seminole elder tells a story.

Children

Seminole children helped with chores. But, there was plenty of time for play. Boys had a few toys. But soon, they learned to use tools and weapons. It was a Seminole **custom** for a boy's uncle to teach him the ways of his people.

The boys learned to hunt. They also learned to make bows from black locust or hickory wood. And, they learned how to be good human beings, to respect elders, and to live in harmony with nature.

Girls learned from their mothers and grandmothers how to tend the gardens, sew, and care for the babies. Young girls often played house. They had dolls made of **palmetto** and cloth. They made camps of tiny dollhouses and buildings.

Sometimes, the children had to protect the corn from small animals and birds. This was an important job. Crops were important for survival.

Children loved to hear the stories about their **ancestors**. They liked creation stories. They even liked the scary stories. And, they liked stories that taught them valuable lessons.

A boy's uncle teaches him how to hunt.

Myths

One Seminole **myth** tells how the **clans** were created.

After the Creator had made the world, he wanted to create many things to live on Earth. He wanted to make sure that these things were equal, and had special healing abilities.

The panther sat by the Creator's side as he created. The Creator loved to pet his sleek body. By touching the panther, the Creator gave it healing powers. The Creator wanted the panther to be the first to walk on Earth.

The Creator put all his creations inside a large shell. Then, he placed it on a mountain ridge next to a young tree.

The tree began to grow. The tree roots wrapped around the shell. Finally, the roots cracked the shell.

Wind was excited to see the opening. But, the panther did not come out. Wind whirled around and helped the panther become the first to walk on Earth.

Soon, all the animals came out of the shell and took their places on Earth. The creator named the animals and put them into **clans**: Panther, Wind, Bear, Deer, Bird, Snake, Toad, and Otter.

The Creator and the panther

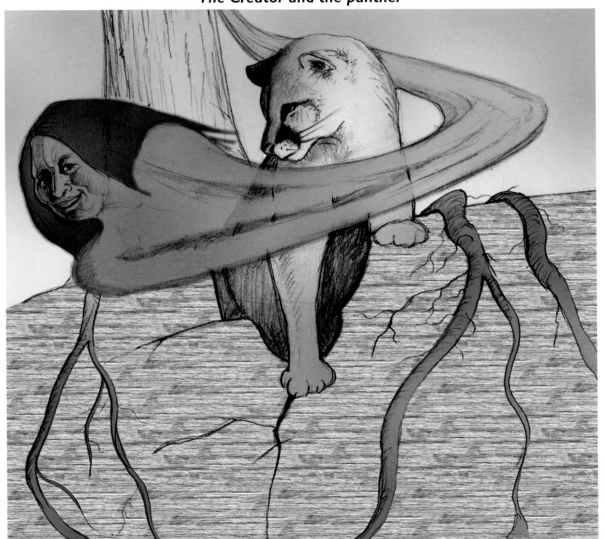

War

Seminole used many types of weapons. They used war clubs spiked with shark teeth. They used spears with bone tips. They used blow guns and darts. And, they used bows and arrows. The arrows were made from river cane. They had flint or bone arrowheads.

After the Europeans arrived in America, Seminole weapons changed. Arrowheads were made of metal. They also began to use guns.

During the Creek War of 1812 –1814, General Andrew Jackson attacked the Seminole in Georgia and Alabama. Many of the Seminole survivors moved to Florida. They wanted to escape the war and the white settlers who wanted their land.

In 1817, Jackson and his troops went to Florida. They began looking for runaway slaves and Seminole relatives who had survived the Creek War.

Jackson's troops burned Seminole villages. Many Seminole were killed. This began the first of the three Seminole Wars that the United States fought. The last war ended in 1858.

In 1830, the Indian Removal Act became law. The act forced many Native Americans to leave their homelands and move to Oklahoma. The Seminole fought bravely against removal. They did not want to leave their homelands.

The Seminole won many battles against the American troops. They never surrendered or signed a peace **treaty** with the U.S. government. Still, about 3,000 Seminole and runaway slaves were moved to "Indian Territory" in Oklahoma. Others remained in Florida where their **descendants** live today.

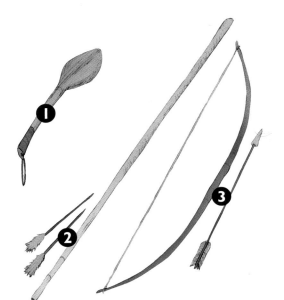

Seminole weapons:
1. War club
2. Darts and blow gun
3. Bow and arrow

Contact with Europeans

In 1513, Spanish explorer Juan Ponce de León arrived on the **peninsula** of present-day Florida. He claimed the land for Spain. Ponce de León made contact with many of the native people there.

In 1539, another Spanish explorer, Hernando de Soto, arrived in Florida. He traveled to present-day Georgia and Alabama in search of gold. De Soto met many Seminole **ancestors**. He tortured and killed them when they did not tell him where to find gold.

The Europeans brought change and misfortune to the Seminole. They had no medicines to cure the diseases they got from the Europeans. Many Seminole died.

Trade was important to the Seminole. They traded with other native peoples for goods they needed to survive. When the Europeans arrived, the Seminole traded with them, too. The Seminole traded deerskins, alligator hides, egret feathers, and dried fish for cloth, coffee, flour, sugar, guns, knives, and brass pots.

The Seminole loaded their trade goods into dugout canoes. Then, they pushed the canoes with long poles. Poling was the best way to steer and move canoes. The swamps were often too shallow for paddling.

European trade goods changed some parts of Seminole **culture**. For example, cloth changed Seminole clothing. The Seminole women began to make beautiful dresses and shirts from **calico** and solid-colored cloth.

Trading goods with a Spaniard

Osceola

Osceola (Asi-yaholo) was a great Seminole leader. He was born in Georgia in 1804. Then, he and his parents moved to Florida when he was four years old.

In the 1830s, the United States tried to force the southeastern Native Americans to move to Indian Territory in present-day Oklahoma. In 1832, some Seminoles signed a **treaty** that would move them to Indian Territory. Osceola was against this treaty. He was arrested for refusing to sign it.

Osceola and **medicine man** Abiaka fought against removal during the second Seminole War. Osceola led the Seminole deeper into the **Everglades**. The swamps and hit-and-run warfare helped the Seminole win many battles against the U.S. Army. But, Osceola was captured and sent to a South Carolina prison. He died there in 1838.

A nineteenth century drawing of Osceola

The Seminole Today

Today, there are seven Seminole **reservations**. One is located in Oklahoma. The other six are in Florida.

The Seminole Nation of Oklahoma has its tribal headquarters in Wewoka. This reservation has about 12,000 members. The Oklahoma Seminole are **descendants** of the native peoples

moved during the late 1830s and early 1840s.

The Oklahoma Seminole are working hard to **preserve** their **culture**. There are programs that teach the Seminole language to Seminole children in the public schools.

The six reservations in Florida are Hollywood, Big Cypress, Immokalee, Tampa, Brighton, and

William Osceola stands next to a chickee.

Fort Pierce. The Seminole Tribe of Florida **reservation** is 90,000 acres (36,000 ha).

The Seminole Tribe of Florida has about 3,000 members. The Florida Seminole are **descendants** of the people who escaped U.S. troops by hiding in the **Everglades**.

The Florida Seminole are also working hard to **preserve** their **culture**. They have a Web site that teaches other people about Seminole culture and history. They also have museums and cultural programs.

Smiling for the camera

At the Big Cypress Reservation, people can visit the Ah-Tah-Thi-Ki Museum. In the Seminole's language, *ah-tah-thi-ki* means "to learn." At the museum, people can see **artifacts**, take guided tours, see a film, and go for nature walks.

A Seminole woman in modern dress

People can also see what life was like for the Florida Seminole. There is a living Seminole village where people demonstrate arts and crafts.

Also at the Big Cypress **Reservation** is the Billie Swamp Safari. People can take a swamp tour on an air boat and see the **Everglade** hammocks and wildlife. And, there's a re-created swamp village. On the night tours, Seminole **elders** tell **legends**. Visitors can stay in a real *chickee*.

Ah-Tah-Thi-Ki Museum director Billy Cypress, center, stands among life-like mannequins. They help show Seminole life at the Big Cypress Reservation.

Glossary

ancestor - a person from whom one is descended.
artifact - anything made by human skill or work.
breechcloth - a simple garment worn by men to cover their loins, a loincloth.
calico - a cotton fabric printed with small, colorful designs.
clan - a group of families who claim descent from the same ancestor.
crescent - shaped like the moon in its first or last quarter.
culture - the customs, arts, and tools of a nation or people at a certain time.
custom - an accepted social habit or behavior of a group.
descendant - a person who comes from a particular ancestor or group of ancestors.
elder - a person having authority because of age or experience.
Everglades - an area of approximately 40 square miles (104 sq. k) of marsh and swamp in southern Florida, the home of many alligators, snakes, and other animals.
extinct - no longer existing.
fiber - a thread-like part.
hominy - kernels of white corn that have been dried and hulled, prepared for eating by being mixed with water and boiled.
legend - a story coming down from the past, which many people have believed.
mantle - a loose cloak without sleeves.
medicine man - a spiritual leader of a tribe or nation.
myth - a legend or story that tries to explain nature.
palmetto fronds - the long fan-like leaves of the palmetto palm tree, used by the Seminole to make roofs for their homes
pendant - a hanging ornament.
peninsula - a piece of land almost surrounded by water.
preserve - to keep from harm or change.
rafter - a slanting beam of a roof.
reservation - a tract of land that is set aside by the government for Native American tribes.
ritual - a form or system of rites.
tradition - the handing down of beliefs, customs, and stories from parents to children.
treaty - a formal agreement between nations.

Web Sites

Seminole Tribe of Florida: **http://www.seminoletribe.com**
Seminole Nation of Oklahoma: **http://www.cowboy.net/native/seminole/index.html**
For information on the National Museum of the American Indian, see the Smithsonian's Web site: **http://www.si.edu/organiza/museums/amerind/abmus/index.htm**

These sites are subject to change. Go to your favorite search engine and type in "Seminole" for more sites.

Index